POEMS and PRAYERS

for CHILDREN

by JOY DEPLEDGE

MOORLEY'S Print & Publishing

ISBN 0 86071 389 X

MOORLEY'S Print & Publishing
23 PARK ROAD, ILKESTON, DERBYS., DE7 5DA - ENGLAND

Gentle Jesus come to me,
Fill my hopeful heart.
Cleanse my soul while I do sleep,
To give me a fresh start.

Another day, another chance,
To prove my human worth.
Gentle Jesus hear the prayers,
Of all your lambs on earth.

■ ■ ■

OUR GIFT

Almost two thousand years ago
A baby Boy was born,
And people came from miles around
That first cold Christmas morn.

His destiny was set to bring
Peace, joy and love to earth,
How could we know the magnitude
Of such a humble birth?

Now, in the twentieth century
When Christmas time is here,
We remember Mary's Boy child
The message is still clear.

Gold, frankincense and myrrh were given
To celebrate His birth,
But the best gift we could give Him now
Would be lasting peace on earth.

■ ■ ■

JESUS

Baby Jesus was born in a stable,
Beneath a bright shining star.
There were angels and shepherds
To greet Him,
And three kings who had travelled afar.

Boy Jesus prayed in the temple,
Joseph and Mary just knew.
That Jesus was special and different,
Into a fine man He grew.

Jesus the Man was a teacher,
With disciples He spoke to the crowds.
He fed them with bread and with fishes,
And He spoke of the Father out loud.

Jesus the Man was a healer,
By the touch of His hand or His hem.
Imagine the joy His healing did bring,
His powers by God they were sent.

Jesus the Man was our saviour,
Nailed to a cross, to our shame.
He died so our sins be forgiven
Amidst hearts full of anguish and pain.

Jesus our Lord and redeemer,
Let all fears and doubts now be ceased.
In heaven we'll meet with our saviour,
Jesus the man, prince of peace.

BEAUTIFUL THINGS

Dear Jesus may we always know
The beauty of this land.
The mountains, seas and rivers
Meadows and golden sands.

■ ■ ■

Animals living in the wild
Plants and flowers which bloom.
Surviving cold and deepest snow
The sun, the stars, the moon.

■ ■ ■

The world is such a lovely place
Filled with wondrous things.
Sunshine, rain and rainbows.
And all the birds who sing.

■ ■ ■

Thank you Jesus for our world
And helping us to see
All things bright and beautiful
Thank you for loving me.

A PRAYER

Bless all the children of our world,
Whatever race or creed.
We're all the same and you're our God,
Forgiveness and love we need.

Help us to grow up to be kind,
To each and everything.
Fair and gentle, quiet and strong,
Your praises we all sing.

Teach us respect and teach us love,
Teach us humility.
To offer the hand of friendship,
Bringing warmth and serenity.

Please may we know when we are wrong,
Teach us to apologise.
Then show us your forgiveness Lord,
Please hear our heartfelt cries.

May we be a good example,
To our sisters and our brothers.
Together we will kneel in prayer,
United with each other.

Please bless my mummy and daddy
Brothers and sisters too.
Keep them safe from harm dear Lord
Help us to know You.

Teach us to be unselfish
and think of others first.
May we learn to see the best in them
And not to see the worst.

Teach us to give a helping hand
A burden we can share.
Oh Father grant your blessings
Please will you hear my prayer?

Bless the little birds that fly,
Into the blue and sunny sky.
Bless the animals, large and small,
Protect them Lord and bless them all.

Bless the flowers and the trees,
Bless the sun, the rain, the breeze.
Bless the rivers and oceans deep,
Bless the fish as they swim and leap.

Bless the mountains towering high,
Heavenward into the sky.
Bless our world and help us care,
For plants and creatures everywhere.

A PRAYER FOR A SICK CHILD

Dear Jesus, I am tired today,
Please touch my hand and help me say
My prayers to ask that I may be
Fit enough to pray to Thee.

Sweet Jesus, bless all those who care,
For poorly children everywhere.
We do not always understand
Stay with me and hold my hand.

Dear Jesus, stay beside my bed,
Hear my prayers sincerely said.
Bless my parents, let them see,
That you will always care for me.

■ ■ ■

SEEDLINGS

I'm like a little seedling
Struggling hard to grow.
Planted firmly in the earth
And Jesus loves me so.

To grow I need the sunshine
Lighting all my days.
Love and faith and courage
Please hear my words of praise.

Seedlings need the summer rain
To nurture and to grow.
So our roots grow strong and steadfast
For Jesus loves us so.

Dig out the weeds which stifle us
Fertile ground they cover fast.
Help me to grow strong and true
Give me the faith that lasts.

■ ■ ■

THE CHRISTMAS STORY

Children of the world will listen
To the tale of long ago.
When a child was born to Mary
In a stable dark and cold.

> *Baby Jesus, sweet and small*
> *But He grew to love us all.*

Shepherds, Kings and wise men travelled
A star on high led the way.
Joseph, Mary, Babe and cattle
In the darkness quietly lay.

> *Baby Jesus, sweet and small*
> *But He grew to love us all.*

Gold and frankincense and myrrh
Gifts from all were brought for Him.
Now we hear the Christmas story
And to Him our thanks we sing.

> *Baby Jesus, sweet and small*
> *But He grew to love us all.*

Bethlehem and angel Gabriel
Welcomed Him that wondrous night
Sweet Lord Jesus, how we love You
Children of the world unite.

IT'S VERY IMPORTANT

It's very important to brush my teeth well
And to finish my homework in time.
It's very important to eat all my meals
And to try to be honest and kind.

It's very important not to be late
And to keep my room tidy and neat
It's very important to help, when I can
And be polite to the people I meet.

It's very important to look out both ways
And to cross busy roads with great care.
But the thing that's most important of all
Is to remember to say all my prayers.

■ ■ ■

THROUGH THE WEEK

Seven days in every week
Beginning with a Sunday.
Dear Lord hear our prayers today
And be with us on Monday.

May we wake and say our prayers
On Monday and on Tuesday.
Fill our hearts and walk with us
Make every day 'Good News Day'.

Keep us on the proper path
On Wednesday, Thursday, Friday.
Straight and narrow no turning off
Lead us to Heaven's highway.

Last of all is Saturday
May we look back and pray.
So next week will be better still
Beginning with a Sunday.

■ ■ ■

A KING WAS BORN

A King was born one Christmas night
When all the world was covered white.
A shining star led the way
An Angel's voice was heard to say:
Unto you is born this night
A Holy Saviour, Jesus Christ.

Lowly manger, warm and dim
So poor a place to welcome Him
And yet He grew to love us all
Still we hear His heavenly call:
Peace on earth goodwill to men
Man will learn to love again.

Gentle Mary, tired and worn
Unto you a Son was born
A special baby, Christ the King
To Thee Lord, our thanks we sing:
Hear us when we kneel to pray
And thank you Lord for each new day.

■ ■ ■

JESUS LOVES US

Sunbeams are special
To me they are kisses,
Sent straight from Heaven
To say God is with us.
Every minute
of every day,
Sunbeams are special
And they're sent to say
Jesus loves us.

■ ■ ■

Jesus loves us, one and all
Not only boys and girls.
He loves all creatures great and small
All around the world.

He loves the busy bumble bee
Caterpillars, spiders
He loves us all, it's plain to see
May His sweet love guide us.

■ ■ ■

I close my eyes and say my prayers
And try to calm my mind.
Try not to think of anything
Just for a little time.

I need to think of all the things
I want to pray for now.
Thank you for my blessings Lord
And will you show me how
To be a better person
To grow up kind and sharing
To learn about living and loving
To be gentle, warm and caring.

Please bless the other children
Wherever they may be
May they learn about Jesus too
And love Him just like me.

■ ■ ■

I LOVE TO HEAR

I love to hear the stories in the Bible
To learn of Jesus and His family.
I can just imagine how things were then,
When Jesus lived and worked in Galilee.

I love to hear about the twelve disciples
And how they worked with Jesus long ago.
I can just imagine how they loved Him
And as they watched Him,
How their faith did grow.

TELL ME

Tell me a story of Jesus
A wonderful tale to be told.
Tell me the story of Ages,
A tale that will never grow old.

I love to know all of the wonders
Surrounding His birth and His life.
Of miracles, faith and the healing
Ending the suffering and strife.

Help me to know and love Jesus
With a love and a power so strong.
Help me to be a good Christian
For I've found where my faith does belong.

A PROMISE

If you make a promise, don't break it.
It's important to keep to your word.
Perhaps it's a struggle to make it
But promises always are heard.

They will fill someone with new hope
When they are filled with despair.
It helps them to look to the future,
Thanks to your comfort and care.

Don't let your promise be broken,
It's your last point of trust with a friend.
A promise is love that is spoken
If you break it, then no-one can mend.

■ ■ ■

CHRISTMAS TIME

The world is covered frosty white
Carols echo through the night
The happiness of Christmas will remain.
Ever after, Children's laughter
Christmas time will always be the same.

The children's stockings hanging there
The christmas tree, no long bare
The toys to prove that Father Christmas came.
Oh morning light, child's delight
Christmas time will always be the same.

Christmas morning bells a ringing
Children's voices sweetly singing
The Christmas Story's ever sweet refrain.
A world of white, Oh silent night
Christmas time will always be the same.

■ ■ ■

EVENING PRAYER

Tightly I close my eyes
And kneel beside my bed.
Hear my prayer sweet Jesus
Even words unsaid.
Help me not to be afraid
Help me not to cry.
Help me to be good and kind
To know the reason why.
Boys and girls should learn to pray
And open up their hearts.
Learn to say a little prayer
Before their slumbers start.

■ ■ ■

MOORLEY'S are growing Publishers, adding several new titles to our list each year. We also undertake private publications and commissioned works.

Our range of publications includes: **Books of Verse**
  Devotional Poetry
  Recitations
  Drama
  Bible Plays
  Sketches
  Nativity Plays
  Passiontide Plays
  Easter Plays
  Demonstrations
  Resource Books
  Assembly Material
  Songs & Musicals
  Children's Addresses
  Prayers & Graces
  Daily Readings
  Books for Speakers
  Activity Books
  Quizzes
  Puzzles
  Painting Books
  Daily Readings
  Church Stationery
  Notice Books
  Cradle Rolls
  Hymn Board Numbers

Please send a S.A.E. (approx 9" x 6") for the current catalogue or consult your local Christian Bookshop who should stock or be able to order our titles.